HOW TO AVOID FLORIDA FORECLOSURE

HOW TO AVOID FLORIDA FORECLOSURE

HOW TO AVOID FLORIDA FORECLOSURE

Mark Galbraith

HOW TO AVOID FLORIDA FORECLOSURE

How to avoid Florida Foreclosure

Copyright © 2010 by Mark Galbraith

ISBN: 1450583350

EAN: 9781450583350

First printing, 2010

Printed in the United States of America

HOW TO AVOID FLORIDA FORECLOSURE

ACKNOWLEDGEMENT

I wish to thank Angel, my wife of 32 years, who provides daily support in my endeavors. She has made it possible for me to have the time to present you this informative and straightforward guide.

I am indebted to her in many ways.

HOW TO AVOID FLORIDA FORECLOSURE

FOREWARD

I have tried to guide Mark in his decision making and his long term goals. His morals, ethics, work habits and the way he treats others have made me proud. My 43 years in real estate were not lost as Mark has expounded on this knowledge in this book to enlighten others on a means to save one's most precious earthly possession. I have tried to set an example by living it and I believe it reflects in his work.

Loren Galbraith
Father

DISCLAIMER

Mark Galbraith is a licensed Realtor® and a licensed Mortgage Broker. Mark Galbraith is NOT a licensed attorney, tax advisor or any other licensed professional.

Nothing in this book is to be taken as legal, financial or tax advice in any way. This information may be inaccurate at time of reading as changes are constantly happening. Please seek appropriate legal or tax advice from a licensed professional.

HOW TO AVOID FLORIDA FORECLOSURE

Introduction

As a Mortgage Broker and a Realtor I have always tried to promote home ownership. It is as they say ..... the American Dream. But for many of us who got caught up in the housing bubble it has become the American Nightmare.

As our economy hit the skids American wage earners are taking home less money each month – if they are still employed. The American home, once one of the safest investments we could make, has become a person's liability rather than their asset. We have experienced one of the worst real estate markets since the depression.

Has your lender started to contact you about past due payments? Are there knots in your stomach because you are so sick over your situation? You must move past the stage of denial that this could never possibly happen to you. Settle down, take a deep breath and then decide you are not going to ignore the problem.

I have gone over every option that I have seen and tried to enlighten the reader on each. I have tried to write this book in easily understood terms. Only in the Appendix will you find government jargon that you will need time to understand.

CONTENTS

HOW TO AVOID FLORIDA FORECLOSURE

HOW TO AVOID FLORIDA FORECLOSURE

What Happened?

Chapter One

Florida is populated mostly by migrants. Less than a third of Floridians were born in the state. Up until a few years ago more people were moving into the state than were leaving (one way or the other). Florida was averaging an increase in population by over a thousand newcomers per day. Our climate, beaches, lakes, recreation, theme parks, relaxed living and low cost of living have attracted many retirees from our Northern states. We also attract heavily from Canada, South America, Cuba and Haiti. The lower value of the dollar started attracting many Europeans who saw how much housing they could get for their money.

Welcome to the Sunshine State!

HOW TO AVOID FLORIDA FORECLOSURE

These people all needed a place to live. This constituted a large driving force for more homes and increased prices. During the height of the market it was a buying frenzy. Homes lasted less than a day on the market. Prices kept being driven up as more people wanted to own a piece of the American Dream and felt they would miss out on a good buying opportunity. For many younger Americans real estate had been a notoriously safe investment. The average yearly increase of real estate value was going gangbusters. One year it exceeded 23% in Florida. Not many safe investments give that kind of return.

How could one lose money in the real estate market?

Most of these homes were purchased with other people's money. The "other people" were banks. And where did banks get their money? A small portion of home loans were backed by the banks' depositors. However, the majority of home loans were sold by these banks on the mortgage resale market and the funds collected were used to finance more home purchases. It was a continual loop where banks made money selling these loans. The more they sold the more money they made. Banks continued to "service" these loans acting as a collection tool for monthly payments and making money on the "servicing" side of the transactions. Most people think because they are making payments to XYZ bank that this bank owns their note. Not true.

So who bought these loans from the banks? In the past home loans were very safe investments. There was a stigma against defaulting on your home loan. People could always sell their home; make a tidy profit and then move up to a better home. Insurance companies were a big player in the purchase of these notes. They rightfully reasoned that these were very safe and gave a good and equitable return on their investments. These notes were rated Triple A, the same as the US government securities.

Then the government wanted more Americans to achieve their American Dream. They helped institute guidelines that were less restrictive for many people who could not otherwise obtain a mortgage. These guidelines were set by Fannie Mae and Freddie Mac, at the time not government run or owned, but rather privately owned and coerced by government influences.

For banks to compete in the market they had to loosen their standards. If they didn't, they wouldn't make the profits that others would. Less profits = less bonuses. Enter the wide acceptance of "sub-prime" lending.

Now other players had entered the re-purchase market. Hedge funds were one of the new players that got into the action.

As could be expected there was a larger default rate of borrowers who had taken out sub-prime mortgages. Hedge funds were one of the first to look at these defaults and "mark down" their investment portfolio. Whoa! After marking down these mortgages the value of any new sub-prime mortgages went way down and there was no longer a market to sell these loans. When the banks have no market to sell loans – they stop making those kinds of loans. Now we start seeing a tightening of credit.

These sub-prime borrowers were a nice chunk of the market. They helped assure the real estate boom. Almost all real estate had a potential buyer. With the lack of these buyers we saw less homes being built and less homes being sold. Homeowners became "stuck" in the homes. Call it the "trickle up" theory.

Add to this mix the negative amortization home loans. Borrowers could purchase a home with little down payment and have a payment that equaled a 1% interest rate with small monthly payments. The balance on these loans grew every year, hence, the name negative amortization loans. They would be good loans for the first five years. Then they would recast and the interest rate would reset at current rates making the payment much larger than what homeowners were accustomed.

And couple in the home loans that would adjust after two years, the adjustable rate mortgages, home loans referred to as ARMs. Again, another home loan with a monthly payment increase. They could then balloon after five years making the entire note due and payable.

Though homeowners should be told at the time of the loan of the changes that would one day come, we all get accustomed to our monthly mortgage payment and budget around this amount. This is just human nature.

The average American held their mortgages for five years (must be a magic number). They either sold and move on or did a refinance.

Now comes the snowball effect. No mortgages because of tight credit means no home sales. No home sales means no home construction. This results in the loss of jobs and has a major impact on the economy. Now the values of homes begin to decline.

Add fuel to the fire: Homeowners Insurance. We are a high risk area. We have the threat of hurricanes. Years 2004 and 2005 hit the insurance industry hard in Florida. Add in wind and water damage, sink holes and even the fear of rising sea levels causes insurance companies to panic. Insurance companies are raising their rates or pulling out. Some have folded up. This leads to a decrease in competition and unfortunately, more rate hikes.

Five years is a long time. So many changes can happen in a family's life within this time frame.

The Correction

Chapter Two

Putting it mildly, it is referred to as a housing market correction. I never imagined we would come close to repeating the crisis of the 1989 Savings and Loan crisis let alone exceed it. Could anyone have envisioned 1929 climate?

We saw investors start to walk away from their deposits on new construction, even if they had put down 20%. Home values eroded quickly. After housing prices peaked around March 2007 they have plummeted.

Where are we headed?

Housing prices will continue to drop until the cost to rent a similar home of comparable size and quality in the same school district is close to cost of owning that same home. Simple math: If you can purchase a home utilizing a mortgage and rent this home out to cover all of your expenses you will know that housing prices have equalized and may be close to swinging in a positive direction. As long as it is cheaper to rent than to buy, we're not there yet.

Do you know anyone who moved out of their home and are now renting a similar home for a lot less than they were paying? Many people are. To some it is a logical business decision. Why pay double for close to the same thing?

Lenders had relaxed their standards to compete and we fell into the trap.

HOW TO AVOID FLORIDA FORECLOSURE

Homeowner Intentions

Chapter Three

Decisions....   Decisions....   Decisions....

A true personal analysis is needed before you do anything.

One of the first items you need to address will be what your intentions are concerning your home. Would you like to stay in your home or is it time to move on? In either case you should consider a time frame for staying. That time frame should either be short term or long term.

Did you build your home? Is there sentimental value attached, such as your great grandparents once owned the home or is this the home where you were born? Do you and your family have all your friends close by and you do not want to upset the children? Do you just love the area because you know it well and have gotten so accustomed to this particular area? The neighbors are just great? Is this your dream home with all the amenities that you desire?

Did you buy the home as an investment property with the hopes of one day selling and making money on the investment? Did you purchase the home because mortgages were cheap and easily obtained and you just knew the property value would go up because it had for so many consecutive years? Did you get caught up in the real estate frenzy that had made millionaires of so many and were inundating late night TV with their success stories?

The next item to consider is what has happened in your life that resulted in your current predicament. Is it temporary? Are you going through a divorce and have run up temporary legal bills? Did you have a medical situation that is now resolved? Did you have an employment change resulting in a temporary loss of income and are now back at the income level you were before the occurrence?

Or is it more permanent? You lost your job and see no hope in the near future for obtaining new employment at the pay level you were accustomed? Your wages have been cut and you see no possibility in the near future to getting back to where you were? You had a medical setback that has left you or another wage earner physically unable to bring home the wages you were making? A divorce has left you as the single payer for the mortgage with only one good source (yours) to pay the bills? Have you become disabled and are still waiting for disability to start to have any income?

The chances are that if you are reading this book then your home is valued at less than you currently owe on your home loan(s). You may be seeing new neighbors moving in that are purchasing a similar home for half or even less than what you currently owe. You may be hearing friends talk of purchasing a home that is nicer than yours for much less money. This only adds to the disillusionment of wanting to stay at the current mortgage value, rate and payment.

But you need to be a realist to determine if you can now afford your home. The following is a quick worksheet so that you can put down in writing what reflects your current expenses. Take the time to write them down. This is an important step in being a realist.

HOW TO AVOID FLORIDA FORECLOSURE

Monthly Expense Worksheet

For this page and the next page - to the right of the expense, put in the dollar amount that you typically pay each month per each expense. If zero, leave blank. Then total both pages.

Mortgage	$
2nd Mortgage	
HOA Dues	
Alimony / Child Support	
Elderly Care	
Auto Loan #1	
Auto Loan #2	
Auto Insurance	
Health Insurance	
Medical Bills	
Life Insurance	
Student Loans	
Automobile Gas	

HOW TO AVOID FLORIDA FORECLOSURE

Automobile Maintenance	$
Groceries	
Entertainment	
Credit Card Bill #1	
Credit Card Bill #2	
Credit Card Bill #3	
Credit Card Bill #4	
Credit Card Bill #5	
Pet Care	
Electricity / Home Gas	
Cable TV	
Home Phone	
Cell Phones	
Sewer / Water	
Internet Service	
Personal Loans	
Other	
Other	
Other	
TOTAL:	

These monthly expenses usually total up to an amount you did not realize were so high. But every little item adds up.

Now take your monthly income from all sources. Use your *take home* pay. This is the amount you actually receive after taxes and other deductions. This includes overtime, commissions and bonuses. Add in any other source of income such as disability or social security.

Then subtract out your total monthly expenses.

Is there anything left over?

This small exercise should enlighten you on what options you should seek.

Communication

Chapter Four

The very first thing you want to do after knowing your expenses and assessing your particular situation is to talk with your lender(s). Do not ignore the problem! Yes, calling the bank can be a very big hassle. Many lenders have now extended hours to accommodate the 9 to 5 worker. Do not be embarrassed. Many people are in the same boat.

Communication is essential to the lender(s). They need to know what is going on and what the homeowner's intentions and abilities are. If they have no sense of what is happening they will act quickly.

HOW TO AVOID FLORIDA FORECLOSURE

Open all mail and correspondence from your lender(s). Return their phone calls. Don't get frustrated. Have patience.

If you are not responding to the lender's phone calls or your phone has been disconnected or you have a new phone number or you have gone to using just your cell phone and the bank is not aware of which phone number to get in touch with you they may send someone out to your home to get in touch with you. This person may take a picture of the outside of your home to prove to the bank they were actually there and verify the home is still standing and not suffering from a disaster (fire, flood etc.). They may try to talk with you or leave a confidentially marked envelope containing a note asking you to call the lender at your door.

The lender also wants to confirm that the home is occupied. An unoccupied home is an invitation for disaster. If they find it unoccupied the lender may take the step of securing the home by changing out the locks and making sure there are no hazards to the community.

When calling the lender, you may call and be put on hold. You may talk with many different people. You may even be on the phone a couple hours at a time. You may have to repeat your story over and over again. You may find that they lose your paperwork. You may get conflicting information. You may feel the right hand doesn't know what the left hand is doing. With all that being said – BE PATIENT! And always follow up within a short period of time to insure they received any paperwork you have sent them.

Be honest with the lender. Tell them what has happened that caused your particular situation. They will try to work something out with you. Listen to their options.

After accessing the lenders options, sit down and see if you can reasonably accept their terms.

...and yes, there are times when nothing can be worked out.

HOW TO AVOID FLORIDA FORECLOSURE

 **BEWARE !**

Chapter Five

It seems hard times bring out the worst in people. Bad times also bring out bad people.

If possible, try to avoid foreclosure prevention or loss mitigation companies. When you fall behind in your mortgage payments you will most likely be contacted by many individuals promising to help. Proceed with Caution! Watch out for any high-pressure sales tactics. If they ask you to sign anything, have them leave you all the paperwork so you can read and understand thoroughly at your leisure before signing. Avoid the Scam! Consult with a professional before signing anything.

Florida law requires that a written contract must be executed by both parties before the consultant can initiate services. The contract must contain specific terms and conditions, a specific notice of the homeowner's right to cancel and other disclosures.

Florida law also prohibits businesses or individuals from collecting up-front fees from the homeowner prior to completing all services contained in the contract. Hence, never pay ANY money up-front. This includes foreclosure rescue services or loan modification services related to foreclosures. This law applies to all businesses located within the state and to out-of-state businesses that provide services to Florida consumers.

Another Caution: What happens if you obtain a loan modification from utilizing one of these companies but you are not happy with the results? What if the new payment schedule still keeps you under water and you know you cannot afford to keep making the new payment schedule? Again, if you go this route you must set criteria beforehand that you can afford.

Beginning January 1, 2010, any individual or company that provides loan modification services must have an active license from the Florida Office of Financial Regulation. This new provision further enhances the Foreclosure Rescue Fraud Prevention Act, which prohibits individuals and businesses from collecting up-front fees for loan modification services related to foreclosures.

Loan modifications can be performed by the homeowners themselves. Their only cost is the time involved and minor copying and mailing charges. It is also advised to consult with a HUD approved counselor before proceeding. These services are free.

HOW TO AVOID FLORIDA FORECLOSURE

The following Florida Statutes apply and protect homeowners:

501.1377 Violations involving homeowners during the course of residential foreclosure proceedings.

501.212 Application

If a homeowner feels they have been scammed, they can contact the Florida Attorney General's office at 1-866-9-NO-SCAM.

What is Foreclosure?

Chapter 6

Foreclosure can happen to anybody - no matter whom they are or where they live. Foreclosure knows no social or financial boundaries. Foreclosure does not discriminate.

The foreclosure process begins when the homeowner fails to make payments of the money due on their mortgage at the appointed time. It is the means in which a lending institution can repossess your home when payments are not made.

After a homeowner misses a payment the lender usually sends out a late notice. When the homeowner misses another payment the lender usually attempts to contact the homeowner by mail and via a phone call to resolve the situation. If no arrangements have been made and the homeowner continues to miss payments, the lender will issue demand for payment under the note in full, based on the acceleration clause. Since most mortgage notes contain language which basically says if the borrower fails to pay the lender under the terms of the note with monthly payments as promised the lender can accelerate the note, meaning that the full amount is due on demand.

Lenders typically do not begin the official foreclosure proceedings until the homeowner is three (3) months past due on their mortgage payment. It is not until the lender actually hires an attorney and files the foreclosure paperwork in the court system that you are officially in foreclosure.

Florida is currently a judicial state. Foreclosure must proceed through our court system. Individuals in the State Legislature have talked about changing this but the current environment is so against banks that I do not see this happening. It would swing the hardship even more so on the homeowner.

After the third missed mortgaged payment the bank has an attorney file a foreclosure motion with the courts known as a lis pendens (lease pen-dense). This is a written notice that a lawsuit has been filed which concerns the title to real property or some interest in that real property. The lis pendens is filed with the clerk of the court, certified that it has been filed, and then recorded with the county recorder. This gives notice to the defendant who owns the real estate that there is a claim on the property, and the recording informs the general public that there is this potential claim against it. The lis pendens must include a legal description of the real property, and the lawsuit must involve the property.

The courts notify the homeowner by means of a summons. If the property has a tenant living in it, they will be served notice. This is a notice that they intend to sell your property, terminate all your rights in that property and evict you from the premises.

Florida Statutes governing foreclosure are found in Chapter 702; FORECLOSURE OF MORTGAGES, AGREEMENTS FOR DEEDS, AND STATUTORY LIENS. I have included the most recent at the end of this book.

HOW TO AVOID FLORIDA FORECLOSURE

The Hardship Letter

Chapter 7

When communicating with your lender they need to know what has changed in your life to cause the inability to meet your obligation. They will need this in writing. It is not as painful as you imagine. This can be typed or even handwritten. Let them know what changed and when these circumstances started. Advise them if this will be temporary or permanent. This is an opportunity to appeal to them to give you another chance. Do not use this letter to complain on the way they have treated you. They will need your name, loan number, the current date and signatures of all who signed the mortgage note. This should be in your own words. Most of all – be honest.

HOW TO AVOID FLORIDA FORECLOSURE

Some common reasons given for hardship (but not limited to) are:

- Loss of job
- Unemployment
- Reduced income
- Failed business
- Divorce or separation
- Too much debt
- Mortgage payment increase (can be caused by rate increase, homeowners insurance or taxes)
- Medical Bills
- Hospitalization
- Illness
- Job relocation
- Death of a co-borrower
- Military Duty
- Major damage to the property
- Incarceration

An actual sample hardship letter that was used for a short sale follows:

2-19-2010

To Whom It May Concern:

Regarding my loan #19736501

I am writing to you to approve the short sale of my property due to the following problems which have created financial distress for me.

I am the legal guardian for my grandmother. For 5 years I was her primary Care Taker until 2 years ago when the doctor requested she be placed in a home. I was and still am responsible for payment of all her bills outside of the convalescent home. Also approx 8 months ago my salary was cut $1 an hour. I tried to help a friend out with some bills and subsequently she never paid me back. This placed me in financial distress and made me behind on all my bills. Then my car was wrecked and the engine had to be replaced. Then I had an injury where all the ligaments in my right foot were torn as well as the ligament tore pieces of bone. This created medical bills. At that point the doctor decided I needed major surgery, a hysterectomy as well as a bladder repair. This incurred more medical bills. In Nov a stool shattered on me when I stood on it and ripped the ligaments causing more medical bills.

And first and foremost I am a single mother who receives absolutely no help from my daughters' father. He has never given me any financial or monetary help at all.

Sincerely,

Jane Doe

HOW TO AVOID FLORIDA FORECLOSURE

An actual sample hardship letter that was used for a loan modification follows:

2-19-2010

To Whom It May Concern:

I am writing this letter to explain the bad things that have happened to me. These bad things have made me become late on my payments. I have tried to do everything possible to make ends meet but just can't do it. I want to stay in my home and would appreciate you considering me to do so.

My employer cut my hours last year and I lost all of the overtime I am used to making. I have been making what payments I can by also borrowing on my credit cards. Now I find myself unable to make my full payments.

I have recently taken a second job but need a little time to get caught up. I am hoping you will lower my monthly payments so I can continue to live in my home.

John Doe

Paperwork

Chapter 8

The dreaded paperwork. At times lenders seem worse than the IRS for documentation. Lenders will ask for written documentation to support the case for every homeowner. Even though you have discussed your particular situation with the lender and they have entered it into their "system", be prepared to send them supporting documentation.

This documentation may consist of:

- The Hardship Letter. I have a chapter dedicated to what a hardship letter is and also a couple of samples so you have an idea of what and how to write one.
- Financial Statement. This may be lender specific – so ASK. If your lender needs to send you one there will be a time delay in mailing. This will consist of all your

monthly expenses offset by your monthly income. They may ask you to list all of your assets including 401K funds. Lenders cannot go after your money in a 401K while it is in the fund. However, once pulled out and placed in an FDIC insured institution / bank these funds become fair game.

- Copies of Supporting Documents for Your Hardship. If you have incurred large medical expenses, gather copies of the hospital, doctor and rehabilitation bills. If you have been laid off, ready a copy of your unemployment receipts. If there was a death, have a copy of the death certificate prepared.

- Copies of Two Most Recent Checking and Saving Account Statements. Lenders need to document that there is insufficient monthly money in your accounts to pay your whole mortgage payments. Some lenders ask for front and back of bank issued statements while others settle for customer downloaded copies off of the homeowner's computer. While communicating with your lender verify which will acceptable to them.

- Copies of Your Two Most Recent Paystubs. Prepare copies of these paystubs for all signers to the mortgage – those actually responsible for the note and whose wages were considered when taking out the mortgage.
- Copy of Current P&L Statement. If you are self employed, prepare the latest P&L for the most recent month and make it year-to- date. Have a copy of last year's final P&L ready.
- Copies of Last Year's Tax Return. Copy all schedules just in case. Some lenders may ask you to go back two years.
- Copies of Last Year's W2s. These are probably attached to your tax returns. Be

prepared to go back two years at the lender's discretion.

- Copy of Divorce Decree. If this is applicable, have a copy ready so they verify this part of the hardship.

Is that enough? You never know. Your lender may ask for other info to support what you have discussed. If you are trying to sell your home they may want copies of information pertaining to how you are trying to sell.

Just be prepared for what they may ask so you only have to make one trip to the copy machine.

When sending documentation to your lender – FOLLOW UP! You don't want to go through all this hassle and find out later they never received the information. Hence, obtain names of who to send the information to and how to send. Will fax be OK? Only by mail? And then ask when you can follow up, whom to follow up with and by what means you can contact this individual.

I cannot stress enough the need to FOLLOW UP!

....and follow up again

Reinstatement

Chapter 9

Your lender may agree to let you pay the total amount you are behind, in a lump sum payment and by a specific date. This amount will get your mortgage caught up immediately, reinstate the mortgage and dismiss the foreclosure.

This total amount due will include the past due payments, late fees, "other fees" and any attorney and court costs the lender has accrued.

These "other" fees can include the lender hiring an outside company to try and contact you, BPO fees, locksmith fees and other fees to secure the property from harming the community, such as draining a pool and securing it from being a nuisance.

A BPO is a Broker's Price Opinion. It is usually done by a licensed Real Estate Agent or Broker and is typically less money than an actual appraisal. This gives the lender an idea of what their collateral is worth.

The reinstatement dollar figure can all add up to be quite a sizable amount of money.

Forbearance

Chapter 10

Do you see light at the end of the tunnel? Are you going to receive an inheritance, large tax refund, some lottery winnings, an increase in wages or re-employment or you are able to cash out some investments? If so, discuss with your lender the possibility of the forbearance option.

Your lender will allow you to reduce your payments or delay them for a short period of time with the understanding that after this short period of time they will receive an agreed upon amount of money. They most likely will need written documentation demonstrating where these funds will be coming and at what given date.

Again, this constitutes communicating effectively with your lender.

Repayment Plan

Chapter 11

This appears to be the most common sense way of resolving mortgage deficiency. A Repayment Plan allows the homeowner to repay part of their delinquent amount each month along with their regular mortgage payment.

Your lender may ask for a sizable amount, maybe even half of the past due amount, to be paid at the start of this work out solution. The time period for repayment is usually from one year to two years.

The Repayment Plan is considered by lenders when the homeowner has suffered a temporary financial setback and is now back on their feet and need a little time to get caught up on payments.

You will most likely need to provide to your lender written documentation as to what caused the setback, utilize the hardship letter, and written documentation as to what means will be utilized to pay the normal monthly payment and the extra past due amounts combined.

The Repayment Plan will eventually put you on track with your monthly mortgage payments.

Again, good communication with your lender is required.

Deferment

Chapter 12

A Mortgage Deferment is utilized when the homeowner becomes delinquent on their payments. Your lender will allow you to tack on missed payments, or "defer" these payments, to the end of the loan. All other conditions of the mortgage stay the same. This will add to the length of the mortgage.

The homeowner will need to make these deferred payments at the end of the deferral period or when the loan is paid off or the home is sold.

There may be additional costs to doing this and your lender should provide a written statement as to what is all involved and what costs are added.

Short Refinance

Chapter 13

Let me preface this chapter with the fact that
homeowners may have the option of doing a
regular refinance. This option is very limited.
The homeowner would have to most likely seek
out a different lender and have sufficient equity
in the home. Most homeowners in default are
either upside down in their home value or close
to it. The real kicker is that the homeowner will
need to have fairly good credit. For every
missed mortgage payment the homeowner's
credit score (FICO) deteriorates rapidly. The
homeowner would also need documented
income. There are very few "no doc" loans
available today. The homeowner should make a
call to a reputable mortgage company and see if
this is an option.

HOW TO AVOID FLORIDA FORECLOSURE

The short refinance or short refi as it has been coined involves your lender writing a new mortgage based on the current market value of your home. The difference in the dollar amount of the old mortgage and the new mortgage is recovered by the lender when the property is eventually sold. The equity you build up in your home will first go to your lender to recover this amount.

Some lenders will take an immediate loss on this difference and write it off reporting a deficiency on your record. Your lender may even allow another lender to refinance your mortgage at the current market value and again take an immediate loss and report a deficiency on your record.

In either case your lender has basically done a short sale of your home back to yourself.

The requirements are very stringent to qualify for this program. Some lenders will not allow any missed payments as the first requirement.

HOW TO AVOID FLORIDA FORECLOSURE

Once viewed as a viable option I have found
extremely few lenders willing to go this route.

HOW TO AVOID FLORIDA FORECLOSURE

Home Affordable Refinance Program

Chapter 14

The government has introduced a program called the Home Affordable Refinance Program. This program allows homeowners the privilege of refinancing if they meet certain conditions.

All servicers for loans owned or guaranteed by Fannie Mae and Freddie Mac are required to participate. Additional servicers are strongly encouraged to participate.

The homeowner's mortgage note must be held by Fannie Mae or Freddi Mac. The homeowner must be current on their mortgage payments (the homeowner cannot have been 30 days late on any mortgage payment over the past 12 months). The homeowner's mortgage balance may not exceed 125% of the home's current market value. This last requirement throws a lot of homeowners out of qualifying as housing values have plummeted.

If you believe you can qualify for this program more info can be found at the "www.makinghomeaffordable.gov" web site or by calling their hotline at 1 -888-995-HOPE.

Loan Modification

Chapter 15

Let's open a can of worms.

This is one of the most talked about solutions to preventing homeowner foreclosure. It is also one that needs to ALWAYS be addressed with your lender before considering moving out of your home. It is also a solution that continues to change.

As with any of the solutions to avoiding home foreclosure this one is totally voluntary by your lender. Again, can I emphasize this enough? Communicate with your lender!

A loan modification will change your existing mortgage note and give you a fresh start managing your payments. This will bring your account up to date almost immediately.

HOW TO AVOID FLORIDA FORECLOSURE

The lender will reduce the Loan Modification note rate to the current Market Rate or lower. I have actually seen some 2% note rates.

Legal fees and related foreclosure costs for work actually completed and applicable to the current default episode may be capitalized into the modified principal balance.

The lender will then re-amortize the total unpaid amount due over a 360 month period from the due date of the first installment required under the modified mortgage.

Hence, the balance will not go but will actually go up. The homeowner will eventually end up paying more on the modified mortgage than the original mortgage. But the interest rate will go down and the payments will go down and give the homeowner the opportunity to stay in their home by reducing the total overall monthly mortgage payment.

Home Affordable Modification Program

Chapter 16

The government has introduced another program referred to as the Home Affordable Modification Program.

All servicers for loans owned or guaranteed by Fannie Mae and Freddie Mac are required to participate. Additional servicers are strongly encouraged to participate.

Some of the requirements include:

- The home must be an owner occupied
- A single family 1-4 unit property (including condominium, cooperative, and manufactured home affixed to a foundation and treated as real property under Florida State Law)

HOW TO AVOID FLORIDA FORECLOSURE

- The home must be a primary residence (verified with tax return, credit report, and other documentation such as a utility bill).
- The home may not be investor-owned.
- The home may not be vacant or condemned.
- Have an unpaid principal balance that is equal to or less than:
  - 1 Unit: $729,750
  - 2 Units: $934,200
  - 3 Units: $1,129,250
  - 4 Units: $1,403,400
- Have a first lien mortgage that was originated on or before January 1, 2009
- Have a monthly mortgage payment (including taxes, insurance and homeowners association dues) greater than 31% of your monthly gross (pre-tax) income

- Have a mortgage payment that is not affordable due to a financial hardship that can be documented

Every potentially eligible borrower who calls or writes in to their servicer in reference to a modification must first be screened for hardship. The lender must decide whether the borrower has had a change in circumstances that causes financial hardship, or is facing a recent or imminent increase in the payment that is likely to create a financial hardship. This must be documented by written supporting documents to your hardship.

Lenders are given monetary incentives to comply and are rewarded annually for a short period if they are successful.

The program's guidelines state:

"Participating servicers may not proceed with a foreclosure sale on an eligible loan until the homeowner has been evaluated for HAMP and,

if eligible, a trial modification offer has been made. Participating servicers must use reasonable efforts to contact homeowners facing foreclosure to determine their eligibility, including in-person contacts at the servicer's discretion. Foreclosure sales may not be conducted while the loan is being considered for a modification or during the trial period. Additionally, once a homeowner has entered into a trial period plan by submitting the first trial period payment, the servicer may not take the first legal action to initiate a new foreclosure."

On January 8, 2010, the US Department of Veterans Affairs (VA) released Circular 26-10-2, which provides instructions for modifying VA loans through the Making Home Affordable Program.

"The VA expects servicers to exert all reasonable efforts to assist veteran borrowers in retaining ownership of their homes or mitigating losses

when retention is not possible. Before considering VA HAMP, servicers must first evaluate defaulted mortgages for traditional loss mitigation actions including repayment plans, special forbearances, and traditional loan modifications. If the payments are affordable, then the traditional loss mitigation option will be used to help the veteran retain the home and avoid foreclosure. If none of the loss mitigation options provide an affordable payment, the servicer must evaluate the loan for a VA HAMP modification prior to deciding that the default is insoluble. VA expects servicers to complete all loss mitigation activities expeditiously, including those under review for HAMP modifications. "

HOW TO AVOID FLORIDA FORECLOSURE

Short Sale

Chapter 17

Up to this point I have tried to cover most of the possibilities available to homeowners to avoid foreclosure and still allow the homeowner to remain in their home.

If you are now confronting the realization that no program exists that will keep you in your home and you are determined to move on, the short sale is one of the most preferred options.

The term short sale derives from the fact that the homeowner's lender agrees to take less money on the sale of the property than is currently owed. The lender is thus "short" of their mortgage payoff. And short sales are anything but short in terms of time taken to accomplish.

HOW TO AVOID FLORIDA FORECLOSURE

You should continue to keep the property maintained in an enticing fashion as to make it easily sold. You should be open to allowing prospects to come inside and visualize them living in the property. These are items you will need to work out amongst yourselves and your listing agent.

Lenders prefer a short sale over letting the property go to foreclosure. Basically it is a money thing. They save a lot of money going this route versus the court costs, attorney fees, upkeep fees and eventual sale fees and sales price (much lower sales price at a foreclosure auction than for a short sale). They also do not want to show the property on their books.

If you decide to go this route, interview Realtors® that specialize in short sales. You can sell your property yourself but since there is no way for you to profit from a short sale (one of the lender's stipulation) I advise you to obtain professional assistance. It will not cost you anything (if it does, something's wrong). **If you need a referral, please contact me (my contact information is at the back of the book).** Make sure the Realtor® asks if you have exhausted all other options of staying in your home prior to seeking to sell. Let them review your financial situation and go over the attempts you have previously taken. Have them leave the paperwork after reviewing with you. This will give you time to go over it thoroughly and seek other's advice. Ask your Realtor® to seek a sale where no deficiency judgment is levied against you. This has become increasingly difficult recently, especially when a second mortgage is involved. However, your Realtor® may not know this until the experience is almost all over and everyone is getting ready to close on the transaction. Have them keep you current on the negotiations of the sale with your lender.

If your current bank accounts reflect a lot of money the lender(s) will wonder why you deem you have a hardship. Large bank accounts are a red flag!

If this is your primary residence, the mortgage was for the original purchase and you have proven hardship, your lender most likely will wipe the slate clean after the sale. If you have a second mortgage the negotiations may get tricky. They may ask for more than the first lender is willing to give them. The first lender controls the situation since they have first lien position. The first lien holder actually dictates how much the second lien holder receives from the sale. The homeowner may be required to pick up the difference. The second lien holder may not be happy with what is being dealt them. This is part of the negotiating process. Your main goal is to avoid a deficiency judgment so you can walk away free and clear.

One true curse of death is having either the first note or the second note being sold prior to closing to what I consider to be basically a debt collection agency. They purchase these notes from the lender for pennies on the dollar. They then hold the homeowner for ransom trying to collect as much as possible. This is becoming more common with second lien holders on investment property. They almost always seek a deficiency judgment after the sale. They will always seek more than what the first lien holder allows them and in most cases will ultimately stop the sale transaction from going through to completion. After approximately 120 days of non-payment on a second lien the homeowner runs a good risk of that note being sold.

Remember: it's not over until you sign off on the closing papers. Until then you can still negotiate.

A good short sale involving only one lender will wipe the slate clean of all liens, including judgments against the property, homeowner association dues, property taxes and any other obligation the homeowner has towards the property. Have your Realtor analyze this before you proceed with signing papers.

There may be tax consequences. The Mortgage Forgiveness Debt Relief Act became law on December 20, 2007. This act offers relief to homeowners who would otherwise owe taxes on forgiven mortgage debt after facing foreclosure. Tax relief has been extended covering debts discharged through calendar year 2012. This protection is limited to primary residences. It is advised to consult with a qualified accountant or CPA to see how this will affect your particular situation.

The homeowner should walk away from a short sale with a breath of fresh air and a monkey off their back!

Deed-In-Lieu

Chapter 18

This procedure allows you to transfer your property voluntarily to your lender and your debt or deficiency is often but not necessarily forgiven. This involves you signing over your home directly to the lender and sending them the keys.

I frown wholeheartedly upon this option. You are basically giving up. Try not to go this route. I haven't ever seen the benefit to the homeowner of doing a deed in lieu of foreclosure. If you are even thinking of going down this avenue contact me and I will put you in touch with a qualified Realtor® to present other possible options.

If you contact your lender ahead of time they may insist that you list your home with a sales agent for a certain period of time before they would even accept your keys. Your lender is not in the real estate business and doesn't want the responsibility of taking possession of your home and then trying to sell it on the market. They would prefer you enjoy this endeavor.

Bankruptcy

Chapter 19

Bankruptcy is a court process designed to help people eliminate their debts or repay them under the protection of the bankruptcy court.

If you are considering going this route – do not be embarrassed. This is a legitimate way afforded homeowners to obtain debt relief.

There are two types of bankruptcy that pertain to individuals. They are referred to as Chapter 13 and Chapter 7.

Under Chapter 13 you obtain a feasible plan for repaying your debts. This plan is put together by you and your attorney and then submitted to the Court. Once accepted, you make monthly payments to the Bankruptcy Trustee. This monthly payment will include your regular mortgage payment plus an additional amount to get the homeowner caught up. The additional amount will include all the past due payments and other fees. These additional fees should be at 0% interest. You may be able to also obtain a lower interest rate on your mortgage payments.

During this time your lender cannot take your home, nor are they allowed to talk with or contact you. Once you have caught up the bankruptcy ends. The maximum time for this to be resolved is 60 months (5 years). Once resolved you go back to making your monthly mortgage payments.

Does this always work? No. If you are unemployed or otherwise have no means to adhere to your plan - your lender will once again seek foreclosure. Also, making payments to the Trustee are time sensitive. Discuss with your attorney what may happen if you are late on any given payment.

HOW TO AVOID FLORIDA FORECLOSURE

Chapter 7 will not save a house from foreclosure if you are delinquent in payments. Under the new bankruptcy law, only people who pass the "means test" may file a Chapter 7 bankruptcy. People who fail the "means test" have to file Chapter 13 bankruptcy provided you are under Chapter 13 debt ceilings. The "means test" is best administered by your attorney.

Bankruptcy is not the right way to go for all individuals. My opinion is that it should be a last resort depending upon your particular situation. Though allowed, I do not consider it a DIY (do it yourself) endeavor. My first inquiry would be to a qualified accountant or CPA to discuss this matter. The fee, if any, should be minimal. If determined that bankruptcy is the proper avenue to go they can then recommend a qualified bankruptcy attorney. A bankruptcy attorney's fee can run upwards of $5,000. You will also need to add in court filing fees.

HOW TO AVOID FLORIDA FORECLOSURE

Florida bankruptcy laws are unique to Florida. If you are a permanent resident of the State of Florida, consult an attorney who can handle Florida bankruptcies. If you are a legal resident of another state, contact an attorney in your state.

The Florida Bar, 651 E. Jefferson Street, Tallahassee, FL 32399-2300 (850) 561-5600 can give you names. Also, the Florida Bar Lawyer Referral Service provides referrals to attorneys who will conduct an initial one-half hour office consultation for $25. They can also give names for attorneys in other states. They can be contacted at 1-800-342-8011.

Moving?

Chapter 20

If you are considering an option that involves you eventually moving out of your home, you will need a place to go. Give this some thought. Will you move in with relatives? Will you move out of the area? Will you rent a home or an apartment? Will you need assistance?

The Florida Department of Children and Families offers a program referred to as the Emergency Financial Assistance for Housing Program. They can be reached at The Department of Children and Families, Office on Homelessness – PDHO, 1317 Winewood Blvd., Tallahassee, FL 32399-0700 Phone: 1-877-891-6445.

HOW TO AVOID FLORIDA FORECLOSURE

The following web site has many resources available in Florida for subsidized housing.

www.hud.gov/local/index.cfm?state=fl&topic=renting

And consider your pets. Will they be accepted at your new locale?

Stress

Chapter 21

Going through financial problems can easily induce stress in a homeowner. This can spread to your loved ones who feel it in you.

Stress and health are closely linked. It is known that stress can induce risky human disorders. Disorders such as high blood pressure, anxiety, tension, crabbiness, sleeplessness and even dizzy spells can be caused by stress and lead to further long term more serious problems.

Watch your stress levels and make sure you keep them reasonable. Exercise is a good stress reliever. If you feel stress getting the best of you and you cannot keep your stress levels maintained - see a physician as soon as possible.

HOW TO AVOID FLORIDA FORECLOSURE

Appendix A

Florida Statute
CHAPTER 702

FORECLOSURE OF MORTGAGES, AGREEMENTS
FOR DEEDS, AND STATUTORY LIENS

702.01 Equity.

702.03 Certain foreclosures validated.

702.035 Legal notice concerning foreclosure
proceedings.

702.04 Mortgaged lands in different counties.

702.05 Mortgaged lands sold for taxes.

702.06 Deficiency decree; common-law suit to
recover deficiency.

702.065 Final judgment in uncontested
proceedings where deficiency judgment waived;
attorney's fees when default judgment entered.

702.07 Power of courts and judges to set aside foreclosure decrees at any time before sale.

702.08 Effect of setting aside foreclosure decree.

702.09 Definitions.

702.10 Order to show cause; entry of final judgment of foreclosure; payment during foreclosure.

702.01 Equity.--All mortgages shall be foreclosed in equity. In a mortgage foreclosure action, the court shall sever for separate trial all counterclaims against the foreclosing mortgagee. The foreclosure claim shall, if tried, be tried to the court without a jury.

History.--RS 1987; GS 2501; RGS 3844; CGL 5747; s. 7, ch. 22858, 1945; s. 2, ch. 87-217.

702.03 Certain foreclosures validated.--All mortgage foreclosures heretofore made, or now pending, wherein there has been annexed to the bill of complaint in such cause, an uncertified copy of the mortgage, as provided by chapter 12095, Acts of 1927, entitled: "An act to amend section 3845 RGS relating to complaint in foreclosure of mortgages" are hereby validated and confirmed insofar as they relate to the copy of the mortgage attached to such complaint, to the same extent and effect as if section 3117, RGS, had been expressly repealed by chapter 12095, 1927, entitled: "An act to amend section 3845 RGS relating to complaint in foreclosure of mortgages."

History.--s. 1, ch. 13642, 1929; CGL 1936 Supp. 5748(1).

702.035 Legal notice concerning foreclosure proceedings.--Whenever a legal advertisement, publication, or notice relating to a foreclosure proceeding is required to be placed in a newspaper, it is the responsibility of the petitioner or petitioner's attorney to place such advertisement, publication, or notice. The advertisement, publication, or notice shall be placed directly by the attorney for the petitioner, by the petitioner if acting pro se, or by the clerk of the court.

History.--s. 4, ch. 2001-215.

702.04 Mortgaged lands in different counties.--When a mortgage includes lands, railroad track, right-of-way, or terminal facilities and station grounds, lying in two or more counties, it may be foreclosed in any one of said counties, and all proceedings shall be had in that county as if all the mortgaged land, railroad track, right-of-way, or terminal facilities and station grounds lay therein, except that notice of the sale must be published in every county wherein any of the lands, railroad track, right-of-way, or terminal facilities and station grounds to be sold lie. After final disposition of the suit, the clerk of the circuit court shall prepare and forward a certified copy of the decree of foreclosure and sale and of the decree of confirmation of sale to the clerk of the circuit court of every county wherein any of the mortgaged lands, railroad tracks, right-of-way, or terminal facilities and station grounds lie, to be recorded in the foreign judgment book of each such county, and the costs of such copies and of the record thereof shall be taxed as costs in the cause.

History.--RS 1989; s. 1, ch. 4420, 1895; GS 2503; s. 1, ch. 7339, 1917; RGS 3846; CGL 5749.

702.05 Mortgaged lands sold for taxes.--Any person who has a lien by mortgage or otherwise upon lands sold for taxes may, within the time allowed by law for redemption, redeem such lands, and the receipt of the officer authorized to receive the amount paid for redemption money shall entitle the lienholder to collect the said amount, with interest at the rate of 10 percent per annum, as a part of and in the same manner as the amount secured by her or his original lien.

History.--s. 1, ch. 3903, 1889; RS 1990; GS 2504; RGS 3847; CGL 5750; s. 783, ch. 97-102.

702.06 Deficiency decree; common-law suit to recover deficiency.--In all suits for the foreclosure of mortgages heretofore or hereafter executed the entry of a deficiency decree for any portion of a deficiency, should one exist, shall be within the sound judicial discretion of the court, but the complainant shall also have the right to sue at common law to recover such deficiency, provided no suit at law to recover such deficiency shall be maintained against the original mortgagor in cases where the mortgage is for the purchase price of the property involved and where the original mortgagee becomes the purchaser thereof at foreclosure sale and also is granted a deficiency decree against the original mortgagor.

History.--s. 1, ch. 11993, 1927; CGL 5751; s. 1, ch. 13625, 1929.

702.065 Final judgment in uncontested proceedings where deficiency judgment waived; attorney's fees when default judgment entered.--

(1) In uncontested mortgage foreclosure proceedings in which the mortgagee waives the right to recoup any deficiency judgment, the court shall enter final judgment within 90 days from the date of the close of pleadings. For the

purposes of this subsection, a mortgage foreclosure proceeding is uncontested if an answer not contesting the foreclosure has been filed or a default judgment has been entered by the court.

(2) In a mortgage foreclosure proceeding, when a default judgment has been entered against the mortgagor and the note or mortgage provides for the award of reasonable attorney's fees, it is not necessary for the court to hold a hearing or adjudge the requested attorney's fees to be reasonable if the fees do not exceed 3 percent of the principal amount owed at the time of filing the complaint, even if the note or mortgage does not specify the percentage of the original amount that would be paid as liquidated damages. Such fees constitute liquidated damages in any proceeding to enforce the note or mortgage. This section does not preclude a challenge to the reasonableness of the attorney's fees.

History.--s. 2, ch. 2001-215.

702.07 Power of courts and judges to set aside foreclosure decrees at any time before sale.-- The circuit courts of this state, and the judges thereof at chambers, shall have jurisdiction, power, and authority to rescind, vacate, and set aside a decree of foreclosure of a mortgage of property at any time before the sale thereof has been actually made pursuant to the terms of such decree, and to dismiss the foreclosure proceeding upon the payment of all court costs.

History.--s. 1, ch. 11881, 1927; CGL 5752.

702.08 Effect of setting aside foreclosure decree.--Whenever a decree of foreclosure has been so rescinded, vacated, and set aside and the foreclosure proceedings dismissed as provided in s. 702.07, the mortgage, together with its lien and the debt thereby secured, shall be, both in law and equity, completely relieved of all effects of any kind whatsoever resulting from or on account of the foreclosure proceedings and the decree of foreclosure and fully restored in all respects to the original status of the same as it existed prior to the foreclosure proceedings and the decree of foreclosure, and thereafter the same shall be for all purposes whatsoever legally of force and effect just as if foreclosure proceeding had never been instituted and a decree of foreclosure had never been made.

History.--s. 2, ch. 11881, 1927; CGL 5753.

702.09 Definitions.--For the purposes of ss. 702.07 and 702.08 the words "decree of foreclosure" shall include a judgment or order rendered or passed in the foreclosure proceedings in which the decree of foreclosure shall be rescinded, vacated, and set aside; the word "mortgage" shall mean any written instrument securing the payment of money or advances and includes liens to secure payment of assessments arising under chapters 718 and 719 and liens created pursuant to the recorded covenants of a homeowners' association as defined in s. 712.01; the word "debt" shall include promissory notes, bonds, and all other written obligations given for the payment of money; the words "foreclosure proceedings" shall embrace every action in the circuit or county courts of this state wherein it is sought to foreclose a mortgage and sell the property covered by the same; and the word "property" shall mean and include both real and personal property.

History.--s. 3, ch. 11881, 1927; CGL 5754; s. 4, ch. 2002-27; s. 13, ch. 2003-14.

702.10 Order to show cause; entry of final judgment of foreclosure; payment during foreclosure.--

(1) After a complaint in a foreclosure proceeding has been filed, the mortgagee may request an order to show cause for the entry of final judgment and the court shall immediately review the complaint. If, upon examination of the complaint, the court finds that the complaint is verified and alleges a cause of action to foreclose on real property, the court shall promptly issue an order directed to the defendant to show cause why a final judgment of foreclosure should not be entered.

(a) The order shall:

HOW TO AVOID FLORIDA FORECLOSURE

1. Set the date and time for hearing on the order to show cause. However, the date for the hearing may not be set sooner than 20 days after the service of the order. When service is obtained by publication, the date for the hearing may not be set sooner than 30 days after the first publication. The hearing must be held within 60 days after the date of service. Failure to hold the hearing within such time does not affect the validity of the order to show cause or the jurisdiction of the court to issue subsequent orders.

2. Direct the time within which service of the order to show cause and the complaint must be made upon the defendant.

3. State that the filing of defenses by a motion or by a verified or sworn answer at or before the hearing to show cause constitutes cause for the court not to enter the attached final judgment.

4. State that the defendant has the right to file affidavits or other papers at the time of the

hearing and may appear personally or by way of an attorney at the hearing.

5. State that, if the defendant files defenses by a motion, the hearing time may be used to hear the defendant's motion.

6. State that, if the defendant fails to appear at the hearing to show cause or fails to file defenses by a motion or by a verified or sworn answer or files an answer not contesting the foreclosure, the defendant may be considered to have waived the right to a hearing and in such case the court may enter a final judgment of foreclosure ordering the clerk of the court to conduct a foreclosure sale.

7. State that if the mortgage provides for reasonable attorney's fees and the requested attorney's fees do not exceed 3 percent of the principal amount owed at the time of filing the complaint, it is unnecessary for the court to hold a hearing or adjudge the requested attorney's fees to be reasonable.

8. Attach the final judgment of foreclosure the court will enter, if the defendant waives the right to be heard at the hearing on the order to show cause.

9. Require the mortgagee to serve a copy of the order to show cause on the mortgagor in the following manner:

a. If the mortgagor has been served with the complaint and original process, service of the order may be made in the manner provided in the Florida Rules of Civil Procedure.

b. If the mortgagor has not been served with the complaint and original process, the order to show cause, together with the summons and a copy of the complaint, shall be served on the mortgagor in the same manner as provided by law for original process.

Any final judgment of foreclosure entered under this subsection is for in rem relief only. Nothing in this subsection shall preclude the entry of a deficiency judgment where otherwise allowed by law.

(b) The right to be heard at the hearing to show cause is waived if the defendant, after being served as provided by law with an order to show cause, engages in conduct that clearly shows that the defendant has relinquished the right to be heard on that order. The defendant's failure to file defenses by a motion or by a sworn or verified answer or to appear at the hearing duly scheduled on the order to show cause presumptively constitutes conduct that clearly shows that the defendant has relinquished the right to be heard. If a defendant files defenses by a motion or by a verified or sworn answer at or before the hearing, such action constitutes cause and precludes the entry of a final judgment at the hearing to show cause.

(c) In a mortgage foreclosure proceeding, when a default judgment has been entered against the mortgagor and the note or mortgage provides for the award of reasonable attorney's fees, it is unnecessary for the court to hold a hearing or adjudge the requested attorney's fees to be reasonable if the fees do not exceed 3 percent of the principal amount owed on the note or mortgage at the time of filing, even if the note or mortgage does not specify the percentage of the original amount that would be paid as liquidated damages.

(d) If the court finds that the defendant has waived the right to be heard as provided in paragraph (b), the court shall promptly enter a final judgment of foreclosure. If the court finds that the defendant has not waived the right to be heard on the order to show cause, the court shall then determine whether there is cause not to enter a final judgment of foreclosure. If the court finds that the defendant has not shown cause, the court shall promptly enter a judgment of foreclosure.

(2) In an action for foreclosure, other than residential real estate, the mortgagee may request that the court enter an order directing the mortgagor defendant to show cause why an order to make payments during the pendency

of the foreclosure proceedings or an order to vacate the premises should not be entered.

(a) The order shall:

1. Set the date and time for hearing on the order to show cause. However, the date for the hearing shall not be set sooner than 20 days after the service of the order. Where service is obtained by publication, the date for the hearing shall not be set sooner than 30 days after the first publication.

2. Direct the time within which service of the order to show cause and the complaint shall be made upon the defendant.

3. State that the defendant has the right to file affidavits or other papers at the time of the hearing and may appear personally or by way of an attorney at the hearing.

4. State that, if the defendant fails to appear at the hearing to show cause and fails to file defenses by a motion or by a verified or sworn answer, the defendant may be deemed to have

waived the right to a hearing and in such case the court may enter an order to make payment or vacate the premises.

5. Require the mortgagee to serve a copy of the order to show cause on the mortgagor in the following manner:

a. If the mortgagor has been served with the complaint and original process, service of the order may be made in the manner provided in the Florida Rules of Civil Procedure.

b. If the mortgagor has not been served with the complaint and original process, the order to show cause, together with the summons and a copy of the complaint, shall be served on the mortgagor in the same manner as provided by law for original process.

(b) The right to be heard at the hearing to show cause is waived if the defendant, after being served as provided by law with an order to show cause, engages in conduct that clearly shows that the defendant has relinquished the right to be heard on that order. The defendant's failure to file defenses by a motion or by a sworn or verified answer or to appear at the hearing duly scheduled on the order to show cause presumptively constitutes conduct that clearly shows that the defendant has relinquished the right to be heard.

(c) If the court finds that the defendant has waived the right to be heard as provided in paragraph (b), the court may promptly enter an order requiring payment in the amount provided in paragraph (f) or an order to vacate.

(d) If the court finds that the mortgagor has not waived the right to be heard on the order to show cause, the court shall, at the hearing on the order to show cause, consider the affidavits and other showings made by the parties appearing and make a determination of the probable validity of the underlying claim alleged against the mortgagor and the mortgagor's defenses. If the court determines that the mortgagee is likely to prevail in the foreclosure action, the court shall enter an order requiring the mortgagor to make the payment described in paragraph (e) to the mortgagee and provide for a remedy as described in paragraph (f). However, the order shall be stayed pending final adjudication of the claims of the parties if the mortgagor files with the court a written undertaking executed by a surety approved by the court in an amount equal to the unpaid balance of the mortgage on the property, including all principal, interest, unpaid taxes, and insurance premiums paid by the mortgagee.

(e) In the event the court enters an order requiring the mortgagor to make payments to the mortgagee, payments shall be payable at such intervals and in such amounts provided for in the mortgage instrument before acceleration or maturity. The obligation to make payments pursuant to any order entered under this subsection shall commence from the date of the motion filed hereunder. The order shall be served upon the mortgagor no later than 20 days before the date specified for the first payment. The order may permit, but shall not require the mortgagee to take all appropriate steps to secure the premises during the pendency of the foreclosure action.

(f) In the event the court enters an order requiring payments the order shall also provide that the mortgagee shall be entitled to possession of the premises upon the failure of the mortgagor to make the payment required in the order unless at the hearing on the order to show cause the court finds good cause to order some other method of enforcement of its order.

(g) All amounts paid pursuant to this section shall be credited against the mortgage obligation in accordance with the terms of the loan documents, provided, however, that any payments made under this section shall not constitute a cure of any default or a waiver or any other defense to the mortgage foreclosure action.

(h) Upon the filing of an affidavit with the clerk that the premises have not been vacated pursuant to the court order, the clerk shall issue to the sheriff a writ for possession which shall be governed by the provisions of s. 83.62.

History.--s. 14, ch. 93-250; s. 3, ch. 2001-215.

Appendix B

Making Home Affordable
Summary of Guidelines

U.S. DEPARTMENT OF THE TREASURY
Washington March 4, 2009

Making Home Affordable *will offer assistance to as many as 7 to 9 million homeowners*, making their mortgages more affordable and helping to prevent the destructive impact of foreclosures on families, communities and the national economy.

The Home Affordable Refinance program will be available to 4 to 5 million homeowners who have a solid payment history on an existing mortgage owned by Fannie Mae or Freddie Mac. Normally, these borrowers would be unable to refinance because their homes have lost value, pushing their current loan-to-value ratios above 80%. Under the Home Affordable Refinance program, many of them will now be eligible to refinance their loan to take advantage of today's lower mortgage rates or to refinance an adjustable-rate mortgage into a more stable mortgage, such as a 30-year fixed rate loan.

GSE lenders and servicers already have much of the borrower's information on file, so documentation requirements are not likely to be burdensome. In addition, in some cases an appraisal will not be necessary. This flexibility will make the refinance quicker and less costly for both borrowers and lenders. The Home Affordable Refinance program ends in June 2010.

The *Home Affordable Modification* program will help up to 3 to 4 million at-risk homeowners avoid foreclosure by reducing monthly mortgage payments. Working with the banking and credit union regulators, the FHA, the VA, the USDA and the Federal Housing Finance Agency, the Treasury Department today announced program guidelines that are expected to become standard industry practice in pursuing affordable and sustainable mortgage modifications. This program will work in tandem with an expanded and improved Hope for Homeowners program.

With the information now available, **servicers can begin immediately to modify eligible mortgages** under the Modification program so that **at-risk borrowers can better afford their payments.** The detailed guidelines (separate document) provide information on the following:

Eligibility and Verification

Loans originated on or before January 1, 2009.

First-lien loans on owner-occupied properties with unpaid principal balance up to $729,750. Higher limits allowed for owner-occupied properties with 2-4 units.

All borrowers must fully document income, including signed IRS 4506-T, two most recent pay stubs, and most recent tax return, and must sign an affidavit of financial hardship.

Property owner occupancy status will be verified through borrower credit report and other documentation; no investor-owned, vacant, or condemned properties.

Incentives to lenders and servicers to modify at risk borrowers who have not yet missed payments when the servicer determines that the borrower is at imminent risk of default.

Modifications can start from now until December 31, 2012; loans can be modified only once under the program.

Loan Modification Terms and Procedures:

Participating servicers are required to service all eligible loans under the rules of the program unless explicitly prohibited by contract; servicers are required to use reasonable efforts to obtain waivers of limits on participation. Participating loan servicers will be required to use a net present value (NPV) test on each loan that is at risk of imminent default or at least 60 days delinquent. The NPV test will compare the net present value of cash flows with modification and without modification. If the test is positive – meaning that the net present value of expected cash flow is greater in the modification scenario – the servicer must modify absent fraud or a contract prohibition.

• Parameters of the NPV test are spelled out in the guidelines, including acceptable discount rates, property valuation methodologies, home price appreciation assumptions, foreclosure costs and timelines, and borrower cure and redefault rate assumptions.

• Servicers will follow a specified sequence of steps in order to reduce the monthly payment to no more than 31% of gross monthly income (DTI).

• The modification sequence requires first reducing the interest rate (subject to a rate floor of 2%), then if necessary extending the term or amortization of the loan up to a maximum of 40 years, and then if necessary forbearing principal. Principal forgiveness or a Hope for Homeowners refinancing are acceptable alternatives.

• The monthly payment includes principal, interest, taxes, insurance, flood insurance, homeowner's association and/or condominium fees. Monthly income includes wages, salary, overtime, fees, commissions, tips, social security, pensions, and all other income.

• Servicers must enter into the program agreements with Treasury's financial agent on or before December 31, 2009.

Payments to Servicers, Lenders, and Responsible Borrowers

The program will share with the lender/investor the cost of reductions in monthly payments from 38% DTI to 31% DTI.

Servicers that modify loans according to the guidelines will receive an up-front fee of $1,000 for each modification, plus "pay for success" fees on still-performing loans of $1,000 per year.

Homeowners who make their payments on time are eligible for up to $1,000 of principal reduction payments each year for up to five years.

The program will provide one-time bonus incentive payments of $1,500 to lender/investors and $500 to servicers for modifications made while a borrower is still current on mortgage payments.

The program will include incentives for extinguishing second liens on loans modified under this program.

No payments will be made under the program to the lender/investor, servicer, or borrower unless and until the servicer has first entered into the program agreements with Treasury's financial agent.

Similar incentives will be paid for Hope for Homeowner refinances.

Transparency and Accountability

Measures to prevent and detect fraud, such as documentation and audit requirements, will be central to the program.

Servicers will be required to collect, maintain and transmit records for verification and compliance review, including borrower eligibility, underwriting, incentive payments, property verification, and other documentation.

Freddie Mac will audit compliance.

Appendix C

Introduction of Home Affordable Foreclosure Alternatives –
Short Sale and Deed-in-Lieu of Foreclosure

(NOTE: THIS HAD NOT GONE INTO EFFECT AS OF THIS WRITING. THIS SUMMARY CONTAINS ONLY THE SUPPLEMENTAL DIRECTIVE AND NONE OF THE EXHIBITS).

Background

In Supplemental Directive 09-01, the Treasury Department (Treasury) announced the eligibility, underwriting and servicing requirements for the Home Affordable Modification Program (HAMP). Under HAMP, the servicers apply a uniform loan modification process to provide eligible borrowers with sustainable monthly payments for their first lien mortgage loans. While HAMP program guidelines are intended to reach a broad range of at-risk borrowers, it is expected that servicers will encounter situations where they are unable to approve a HAMP modification request, a HAMP modification is offered and not accepted by the borrower, or the borrower falls out of a HAMP modification. In these instances, the borrower may benefit from an alternative that helps the borrower transition to more affordable housing and avoid the stigma of a foreclosure.

HOW TO AVOID FLORIDA FORECLOSURE

This Supplemental Directive provides guidance to servicers for adoption and implementation of the Home Affordable Foreclosure Alternatives Program (HAFA). HAFA is part of HAMP and provides financial incentives to servicers and borrowers who utilize a short sale or a deed-in-lieu to avoid a foreclosure on an eligible loan under HAMP. Both of these foreclosure alternatives reduce the need for potentially lengthy and expensive foreclosure proceedings. The options help preserve the condition and value of the property by minimizing the time a property is vacant and subject to vandalism and deterioration. In addition, these options generally provide a substantially better outcome than a foreclosure sale for borrowers, investors and communities.

This Supplemental Directive provides guidance to servicers for adoption and implementation of HAFA for first lien mortgage loans that are not owned or guaranteed by Fannie Mae or Freddie Mac (Non-GSE Mortgages). In order for a servicer to participate in HAFA for Non-GSE Mortgages, the servicer must execute a servicer participation agreement and related documents (SPA) with Fannie Mae in its capacity as financial agent for the United States (as designated by Treasury) to participate in HAMP on or before December 31, 2009. In certain circumstances, Supplemental Directive 09-01 requires participating servicers to consider borrowers for other foreclosure prevention options, including short sale and deed-in-lieu programs. As a result, servicers already participating in HAMP must follow the guidance set forth in this

HOW TO AVOID FLORIDA FORECLOSURE

Supplemental Directive, which provides servicers with the option to determine the extent to which short sales or deeds-in-lieu will be offered under this program. Servicers of mortgage loans that are owned or guaranteed by Fannie Mae or Freddie Mac should refer to the HAFA announcement issued by the applicable GSE. A loan must be HAMP eligible and meet the other requirements stated herein to be eligible for incentive compensation under HAFA.

The effective date of this Supplemental Directive is April 5, 2010. A servicer may elect to implement HAFA prior to April 5, 2010, provided that the servicer is able to collect and report all required information as described in the *Reporting Requirements* section of this Supplemental Directive. Borrowers may be accepted into HAFA if a Short Sale Agreement or DIL Agreement, as described in this Supplemental Directive, is fully-executed by the borrower and received by the servicer on or before December 31, 2012.

To help servicers implement HAFA, this Supplemental Directive covers the following topics:

* Foreclosure Alternatives

* HAFA Consideration

* Evaluation

* Short Sale

* Deed-in-Lieu

* General Terms and Conditions

* Incentive Compensation

115

- Standard Form Documents
- Reporting Requirements
- Compliance

Foreclosure Alternatives

In a short sale, the servicer allows the borrower to list and sell the mortgaged property with the understanding that the net proceeds from the sale may be less than the total amount due on the mortgage. The short sale must be an arm's length transaction with the net sale proceeds (after deductions for reasonable and customary selling costs) being applied to a discounted ("short") mortgage payoff acceptable to the servicer. The servicer accepts the short payoff in full satisfaction of the total amount due on the first mortgage.

In a deed-in-lieu of foreclosure (DIL), the borrower voluntarily transfers ownership of the mortgaged property to the servicer in full satisfaction of the total amount due on the first mortgage. The servicer's willingness to approve and accept a DIL is contingent upon the borrower's ability to provide marketable title, free and clear of mortgages, liens and encumbrances. Generally, servicers require the borrower to make a good faith effort to sell the property through a short sale before agreeing to accept the DIL. However, under circumstances acceptable to the investor, the servicer may accept a DIL without the borrower first attempting to sell the property. With either the HAFA short sale or DIL, the servicer may not require a cash contribution or promissory note from the borrower and must forfeit the ability to pursue a deficiency judgment against the borrower.

Short sales and DILs are complex transactions involving coordination and cooperation among a number of parties including, but not limited to, servicers, appraisers, borrowers (sellers), buyers, real estate brokers and agents, title agencies, and often mortgage insurance companies and subordinate and other lien holders. The HAFA program simplifies and streamlines the use of short sales and DIL options by incorporating the following unique features:

· Complements HAMP by providing viable alternatives for borrowers who are HAMP eligible.

· Utilizes borrower financial and hardship information collected in conjunction with HAMP, eliminating the need for additional eligibility analysis.

· Allows the borrower to receive pre-approved short sale terms prior to the property listing.

· Prohibits the servicer from requiring, as a condition of approving the short sale, a reduction in the real estate commission agreed upon in the listing agreement.

· Requires that borrowers be fully released from future liability for the debt.

· Uses standard processes, documents and timeframes.

· Provides financial incentives to borrowers, servicers and investors.

HAFA Consideration

Each participating servicer must develop a written policy, consistent with investor guidelines, that describes the basis on which the servicer will offer the HAFA program to borrowers. This policy may incorporate such factors as the severity of the loss involved, local market conditions, the timing of pending foreclosure actions and borrower motivation and cooperation.

Servicers must evaluate a borrower for a HAMP modification prior to any consideration being given to HAFA options in accordance with the provisions of Supplemental Directive 09-01 and any supplemental HAMP guidance. Borrowers that meet the eligibility criteria for HAMP but who are not offered a Trial Period Plan, do not successfully complete a Trial Period Plan, or default on a HAMP modification should first be considered for other loan modification or retention programs offered by the servicer prior to being evaluated for HAFA.

In accordance with the provisions of Supplemental Directive 09-01, a loan meets the basic eligibility criteria if all of the following conditions are met:

· The property is the borrower's principal residence;

· The mortgage loan is a first lien mortgage originated on or before January 1, 2009;

· The mortgage is delinquent or default is reasonably foreseeable;

· The current unpaid principal balance is equal to or less than $729,750[1]; and

· The borrower's total monthly mortgage payment (as defined in Supplemental Directive 09-01) exceeds 31 percent of the borrower's gross income.

Pursuant to the servicer's policy, every potentially eligible borrower must be considered for HAFA before the borrower's loan is referred to foreclosure or the servicer allows a pending foreclosure sale to be conducted. Servicers must consider possible HAMP eligible borrowers for HAFA within 30 calendar days of the date the borrower:

· Does not qualify for a Trial Period Plan;

· Does not successfully complete a Trial Period Plan;

· Is delinquent on a HAMP modification by missing at least two consecutive payments; or

· Requests a short sale or DIL.

The date and outcome of the HAFA consideration must be documented in the servicer's file.

Evaluation

If the servicer determines that a borrower is eligible for a HAFA offer based on its written policy and this Supplemental Directive, the servicer must follow the steps below to determine if a short sale or DIL offer will be extended to the borrower.

Borrower Solicitation and Response. If the servicer has not already discussed a short sale or DIL with the borrower, the servicer must proactively notify the borrower in writing of the availability of these options and allow the borrower 14 calendar days from the date of the notification to contact the servicer by verbal or written communication and request consideration under HAFA. If the borrower fails to contact the servicer within the timeframe or at any time indicates that he or she is not interested in these options, the servicer has no further obligation to extend a HAFA offer.

Expected Recovery through Foreclosure and Disposition. Though not a HAFA requirement, it is expected that servicers will, in accordance with investor guidelines, perform a financial analysis to determine if a short sale or DIL is in the best interest of the investor, guarantor and/or mortgage insurer. The results of any analysis must be retained in the servicing file. The HAMP base NPV model does not project investor cash flows from either a short sale or DIL and should be used only to determine borrower eligibility for a HAMP modification.

Use of Borrower Financial Information. Verified borrower financial information obtained in conjunction with HAMP may be relied upon to determine a borrower's eligibility for HAFA. If financial and hardship information is documented and verified, no additional financial or hardship assessment is required by HAFA. However, in accordance with investor guidelines, the servicer may request updated financial information to evaluate the borrower. If a borrower was evaluated for HAMP based on verbal financial data, the servicer may send the borrower a Short Sale Agreement (SSA) and must require the borrower to deliver the financial information required under HAMP when the borrower returns the executed SSA. The servicer must verify a borrower's financial information through documentation and obtain a signed Hardship Affidavit prior to approving a short sale or accepting a DIL under HAFA.

Property Valuation. The servicer must, independent of the borrower and any other parties to the transaction, assess the current value of the property in accordance with the investor's guidelines. The servicer may not require the borrower to pay in advance for the valuation, but may add the cost to the outstanding debt in accordance with the borrower's mortgage documents and applicable law in the event the short sale or DIL is not completed.

Review of Title. The servicer must review readily available information provided by the borrower, the borrower's credit report, the loan file or other sources to identify subordinate liens and other claims on title to determine if the borrower will be able to deliver clear, marketable title to a prospective purchaser or the investor. Although not required by HAFA, the servicer may order a title search or preliminary title report. The servicer may not charge the borrower in advance for any cost incurred in the title review, but may add the cost to the outstanding debt in accordance with the borrower's mortgage documents and applicable law in the event the short sale or DIL is not completed.

Borrower Notice. When a HAFA short sale or DIL is not available, the servicer must communicate this decision in writing to any borrower that requested consideration. The notice must explain why a short sale or DIL under HAFA cannot be offered, provide a toll free telephone number that the customer may call to discuss the decision and otherwise comply with the notice requirements of Supplemental Directive 09-08, *Borrower Notices.*

Short Sale

The HAFA short sale process employs standard form documents and defined performance timeframes to facilitate clear communication between the parties to the listing and sale transaction. Servicers must adhere to the following guidelines in connection with the issuance of an SSA.

Minimum Acceptable Net Proceeds. Prior to approving a borrower to participate in a HAFA short sale, the servicer must determine the minimum acceptable net proceeds (minimum net) that the investor will accept from the transaction. Each servicer must develop a written policy, consistent with investor guidelines, that describes the basis on which the minimum net will be determined. This policy may incorporate such factors as local market conditions, customary transactional costs of such sales, and the amounts that may be required to release any subordinate liens on the property. A servicer's policy for determining the minimum net must be consistently applied for all loans serviced for that investor. The minimum net may be expressed as a fixed dollar amount, as a percentage of the current market value of the property, or as a percentage of the list price as approved by the servicer. Once determined, the servicer must document the minimum net in the servicing file for each property subject to HAFA. After signing an SSA, the servicer may not increase the minimum net requirement until the initial SSA termination date is reached (not less than 120 calendar days). Subsequent changes to the minimum net when the SSA is extended must be documented.

Allowable Transaction Costs. In determining the minimum net, the servicer must consider reasonable and customary real estate transaction costs for the community in which the property is located and determine which of these costs the servicer or investor is willing to pay from sale proceeds. The servicer must describe the costs that may be deducted from the gross sale proceeds in the SSA.

Short Sale Agreement. The HAFA SSA, which is attached as Exhibit A, outlines the roles and responsibilities of the servicer and borrower in the short sale listing process and provides key marketing terms, such as a list price or acceptable sale proceeds and the duration of the SSA. The HAFA Request for Approval of a Short Sale (RASS), which must accompany the SSA, is attached as Exhibit A1. The RASS is submitted to the servicer when an offer is received to provide the terms and conditions of the short sale and together with the sales contract, provides settlement instructions to the settlement agent. Either proactively, or at the request of an eligible borrower, the servicer will prepare and send an SSA to the borrower after determining that the proposed sale is in the best interest of the investor. The servicer will also provide the borrower a RASS, pre-populated with contact information for the servicer, the property address and the loan number.

In the event that a borrower has an executed sales contract and requests the servicer to approve a short sale under HAFA before an SSA has been executed, the servicer must evaluate the borrower for HAFA as described in this Supplemental Directive and must utilize the Alternative Request for Approval of a Short Sale (Alternative RASS).

While servicers may amend the terms of the SSA in accordance with investor requirements, applicable laws or local real estate practice, at a minimum the SSA must include the following:

· A fixed termination date not less than 120 calendar days from the effective date of the SSA ("Effective Date"). The Effective Date must be stated in the SSA and is the date the SSA is mailed to the borrower. The term of the SSA may be extended at the discretion of the servicer up to a total term of 12 months, in accordance with the requirements of the investor.

· A requirement that the property be listed with a licensed real estate professional who is regularly doing business in the community where the property is located.

· Either a list price approved by the servicer or the acceptable sale proceeds, expressed as a net amount after subtracting allowable costs that the servicer will accept from the transaction.

· The amount of closing costs or other expenses the servicer will permit to be deducted from the gross sale proceeds expressed as a dollar amount, a percentage of the list price or a list by category of reasonable closing costs and other expenses that the servicer will permit to be deducted from the gross sale proceeds.

HOW TO AVOID FLORIDA FORECLOSURE

- The amount of the real estate commission that may be paid, not to exceed 6% of the contract sales price, and notification if any portion of the commission must be paid to a contractor of the servicer that has been retained to assist the listing broker with the transaction.

- A statement by the borrower authorizing the servicer to communicate the borrower's personal financial information to other parties (including Treasury and its agents) as necessary to complete the transaction.

- Cancellation and contingency clauses that must be included in listing and sale agreements notifying prospective purchasers that the sale is subject to approval by the servicer and/or third parties.
Notice that the sale must represent an arm's length transaction and that the purchaser may not sell the property within 90 calendar days of closing, including certification language regarding the arm's length transaction that must be included in the sales contract.

- An agreement that upon successful closing of a short sale acceptable to the servicer, the borrower will be released from all liability for repayment of the first mortgage debt.

- An agreement that upon successful closing of a short sale acceptable to the servicer the borrower will be entitled to a relocation incentive of $1,500, which will be deducted from the gross sale proceeds at closing.

- Notice that the servicer will allow a portion of gross sale proceeds to be paid to subordinate lien holders in exchange for release and full satisfaction of their liens.

· Notice that a short sale may have income tax consequences and/or may have a derogatory impact on the borrower's credit score and a recommendation that the borrower seek professional advice regarding these matters.

· The amount of the monthly mortgage payment, if any, that the borrower will be required to pay during the term of the SSA, which amount must not exceed 31% of the borrower's gross monthly income.

· An agreement that so long as the borrower performs in accordance with the terms of the SSA, the servicer will not complete a foreclosure sale.

· Terms under which the SSA can be terminated.

Borrower Obligations. The borrower must sign and return the SSA within 14 calendar days from its Effective Date along with a copy of the real estate broker listing agreement and information regarding any subordinate liens. In returning and signing the SSA the borrower agrees to:

· Provide all information and sign documents required to verify program eligibility.

· Cooperate with the listing broker to actively market the property and respond to servicer inquiries.

· Maintain the interior and exterior of the property in a manner that facilitates marketability.

· Work to clear any liens or other impediments to title that would prevent conveyance.

· Make the monthly payment stipulated in the SSA, if applicable.

Monitoring Marketing Activity / Cause for Termination.

During the term of the SSA, the servicer may terminate the SSA before its expiration due to any of the following events:

· The borrower's financial situation improves significantly, the borrower qualifies for a modification, or the borrower brings the account current or pays the mortgage in full.

· The borrower or the listing broker fails to act in good faith in listing, marketing and/or closing the sale, or otherwise fails to abide by the terms of the SSA.

· A significant change occurs to the property condition and/or value.

· There is evidence of fraud or misrepresentation.

· The borrower files for bankruptcy and the Bankruptcy Court declines to approve the SSA.
Litigation is initiated or threatened that could affect title to the property or interfere with a valid conveyance.

· The borrower fails to make the monthly payment stipulated in the SSA, if applicable.

Request for Approval of Short Sale.

Within three business days following receipt of an executed purchase offer, the borrower or the listing broker must deliver to the servicer a completed RASS describing the terms of the sale transaction. With the RASS, the borrower must submit t o the servicer:

- A copy of the executed sales contract and all addenda.
- Buyer's documentation of funds or buyer's pre-approval or commitment letter on letterhead from a lender.
- All information regarding the status of subordinate liens and/or negotiations with subordinate lien holders.

Approval or Disapproval of Sale.

Within ten business days of receipt of the RASS and all required attachments, the servicer must indicate its approval or disapproval of the proposed sale by signing the appropriate section of the RASS and mailing it to the borrower.

The servicer must approve a RASS if the net sale proceeds available for payment to the servicer equal or exceed the minimum net determined by the servicer prior to the execution or extension of the SSA and all other sales terms and conditions in the SSA have been met. Additionally, the servicer may not require, as a condition of approving a short sale, a reduction in the real estate commission below the commission stated in the SSA.

The servicer may require that the sale closing take place within a reasonable period following acceptance of the RASS, but in no event may the servicer require that a transaction close in less than 45 calendar days from the date of the sales contract without the consent of the borrower.

Alternative Request for Approval of Short Sale.

If the borrower has an executed sales contract and requests the servicer to approve a short sale under HAFA before an SSA has been executed, then the borrower must submit the request to the servicer in the form of the Alternative Request for Approval of Short Sale (Alternative RASS), attached as Exhibit B. Upon receipt of the Alternative RASS, the servicer must determine the basic eligibility of the borrower as described in the *HAFA Consideration* section of this Supplemental Directive. If the borrower appears to be eligible and was not previously considered for a Trial Period Plan, the servicer must notify the borrower verbally or in writing of the availability of a HAMP modification and allow the borrower 14 calendar days from the date of the notification to contact the servicer by verbal or written communication and request consideration for a HAMP modification. In addition, the servicer must verify the borrower's financial information through documentation and obtain a signed Hardship Affidavit from the borrower prior to approving the short sale.

If the borrower does not wish to be considered for a modification, the servicer may consider the Alternative RASS in accordance with this Supplemental Directive without first having to enter into an SSA with the borrower. If the servicer approves the short sale, then the loan will qualify for the HAFA program. A borrower may not participate in a HAMP Trial Period Plan and agree to a HAFA SSA simultaneously. In addition, the servicer must collect and report the information required under Supplemental Directive 09-06 prior to reporting any HAFA information required by this Supplemental Directive.

Deed-in-Lieu

In accordance with investor requirements, servicers have the discretion to accept a HAFA DIL, which requires a full release of the debt and waiver of all claims against the borrower. The borrower must agree to vacate the property by a date certain, leave the property in broom clean condition and deliver clear, marketable title. Typically, servicers require that the borrower make a good faith effort to list and market the property before the servicer will agree to accept a DIL. Under circumstances acceptable to the investor, servicers may agree to accept a DIL without requiring a marketing period. In either circumstance, the transaction will be eligible for incentives as described in the *Incentive Compensation* section of this Supplemental Directive if the borrower meets the HAFA eligibility criteria.

SSA.

The SSA contains optional DIL language that may be included or deleted by the servicer prior to execution of the SSA. If the DIL language is included, the investor is obligated to accept a DIL in accordance with the terms of the SSA if the term of the SSA expires without resulting in a sale of the property. If the servicer offers the DIL option separately from the SSA or without a marketing period, the servicer must provide the Deed-in-Lieu Agreement form ("DIL Agreement"), attached as Exhibit C.

DIL Terms.

The following terms apply to a HAFA DIL:

· **Marketable Title**. The borrower must be able to convey clear, marketable title to the servicer or investor. The requirements for extinguishment of subordinate liens as described in the *Release of Subordinate Liens* section of this Supplemental Directive apply to DIL transactions.

· **Written Agreement**. The conditions for acceptance of a DIL must be in writing and signed by both the servicer and borrower. They may be set forth in the SSA if approved with the short sale, or in the DIL Agreement.

· **Vacancy Date**. The SSA or DIL Agreement must specify the date by which the borrower must vacate the property, which in no event shall be less than 30 calendar days from the date of the termination date of the SSA or the date of a separate DIL Agreement, unless the borrower voluntarily agrees to an earlier date.

· **Relocation Assistance**. Borrowers who participate in a HAFA DIL transaction are eligible for $1,500 in relocation assistance as described in the *Incentive Compensation* section of this Supplemental Directive.

General Terms and Conditions

Suspension of Foreclosure Sales. At the servicer's discretion, the servicer may initiate foreclosure or continue with an existing foreclosure proceeding during the HAFA process, but may not complete a foreclosure sale:

- While determining the borrower's eligibility and qualification for HAMP or HAFA.

- While awaiting the timely return of a fully executed SSA.

- During the term of a fully executed SSA.

- Pending transfer of property ownership based on an approved sales contract per the RASS or Alternative RASS.

- Pending transfer of property ownership via a DIL by the date specified in the SSA or DIL Agreement.

Payment Forbearance. The servicer will identify in the SSA, Alternative RASS or DIL Agreement the amount of the monthly mortgage payment, if any, that the borrower is required to make during the term of the applicable agreement and pending transfer of property ownership, as applicable. In no event may the amount of the borrower's monthly payment exceed the equivalent of 31% of the borrower's gross monthly income. Servicers must develop a written policy in accordance with investor requirements that identifies the circumstances under which they will require monthly payments and how that payment will be determined. Any requirement for the borrower to make monthly payments must be in accordance with applicable laws, rules and regulations.

Release of Subordinate Liens. It is the responsibility of the borrower to deliver clear marketable title to the purchaser or investor and to work with the listing broker, settlement agent and/or lien holders to clear title impediments. The servicer may, but is not required to, negotiate with subordinate lien holders on behalf of the borrower. The servicer, on behalf of the investor, will authorize the settlement agent to allow up to an aggregate of $3,000 of the gross sale proceeds as payment(s) to subordinate mortgage/lien holder(s) in exchange for a lien release and full release of borrower liability. Each lien holder, in order of priority, may be paid three percent (3%) of the unpaid principal balance of their loan, until the $3,000 aggregate cap is reached. Payments will be made at closing from the gross sale proceeds and must be reflected on the HUD-1 Settlement Statement. Investors are eligible for incentive reimbursement for up to one third of the cost to extinguish subordinate liens as described in the *Incentive Compensation* section of this Supplemental Directive.

Release of First Mortgage Lien. The servicer must release its first mortgage lien within ten business days (or earlier if required by state or local laws) after receipt of sale proceeds from a short sale or delivery of the deed and property in a DIL transaction. Additionally, the investor must waive all rights to seek a deficiency judgment and may not require the borrower to sign a promissory note for the deficiency.

Borrower Fees. Servicers may not charge the borrower any administrative processing fees in connection with HAFA. The servicer must pay all out-of-pocket expenses, including but not limited to notary fees, recordation fees, release fees, title costs, property valuation fees, credit report fees, or other allowable and documented expenses, but the servicer may add these costs to the outstanding debt in accordance with borrower's mortgage documents and applicable laws in the event the short sale or DIL is not completed. Servicers may require borrowers to waive reimbursement of any remaining escrow, buy down funds or prepaid items, and assign any insurance proceeds to the investor, if applicable. Those funds will not be applied to reduce the total net proceeds from the sale.

Mortgage Insurer Approval. For loans that have mortgage insurance coverage, the servicer/investor must obtain mortgage insurer approval for HAFA foreclosure alternatives. A mortgage loan does not qualify for HAFA unless the mortgage insurer waives any right to collect additional sums (cash contribution or a promissory note) from the borrower.

Incentive Compensation

Treasury will provide reimbursements and incentives as set forth below. However, no incentives will be paid to the borrower, servicer or investor if the net proceeds from a sale exceed the total amount due on the first mortgage when title is transferred. The amount of any contribution paid by a mortgage insurer or other provider of credit enhancement shall not be considered in determining whether the mortgage was paid in full and whether servicers are eligible for such incentive compensation.

Borrowers, servicers and investors will be eligible for HAFA incentives upon successful completion of the short sale or DIL if an SSA, Alternative RASS or DIL Agreement, as applicable, was executed on or before December 31, 2012. Servicers will be reimbursed by Treasury upon reporting the completed HAFA transaction as described in the *Reporting Requirements* section of this Supplemental Directive. For a short sale or DIL, incentives will be paid as follows:

Borrower Relocation Assistance. Following the successful closing of a short sale or DIL, the borrower shall be entitled to an incentive payment of $1,500 to assist with relocation expenses.

In a short sale transaction, the servicer must instruct the settlement agent to pay the borrower from sale proceeds at the same time that all other payments, including the payoff to the servicer, are disbursed by the settlement agent. The amount paid to the borrower must appear on the HUD-1 Settlement Statement.

If the servicer conducts a formal closing for a DIL transaction and the borrower has vacated the property, the borrower relocation incentive of $1,500 must be paid at closing and reflected on the HUD-1 Settlement Statement. If at the time of closing the borrower has not vacated the property, the servicer must mail a check to the borrower within five business days of the borrower's vacancy and delivery of keys to the servicer or the servicer's agent. Similarly, if the DIL transaction is not conducted as a formal closing, the servicer must mail a check to theborrower within five business days from the later of the borrower's execution of the deed or the borrower's vacancy and delivery of keys to the servicer or servicer's agent.

Servicers will be reimbursed for the full amount of this incentive payment after the HAFA transaction is reported as described in *Reporting Requirements* section of this Supplemental Directive.

Servicer Incentive. The servicer will be paid $1,000 to cover administrative and processing costs for a short sale or DIL completed in accordance with the requirements of HAFA and the applicable documents. Investors may elect to pay additional incentive compensation to servicers which will not affect the HAFA servicer incentive.

Investor Reimbursement for Subordinate Lien Releases.

The investor will be paid a maximum of $1,000 for allowing a total of up to $3,000 in short-sale proceeds to be distributed to subordinate lien holders, or for allowing payment of up to $3,000 to subordinate lien holders. This reimbursement will be earned on a one-for-three matching basis. For each three dollars an investor pays to secure release of a subordinate lien, the investor will be entitled to one dollar of reimbursement. To receive an incentive, subordinate lien holders must release their liens and waive all future claims against the borrower. The servicer is not responsible for any future actions or claims against the borrower by such subordinate lien holders or creditors.

Standard Form Documents

Servicers are required to use the HAFA documents attached to this Supplemental Directive substantially the form provided, except that the servicer may amend the terms of the SSA or DIL Agreement in accordance with investor requirements, applicable laws or local real estate practice and may customize the forms with servicer specific logos.

Document Retention. Servicers must retain all documents and information received during the process of determining borrower eligibility and qualification for HAFA. For a period of seven years from the date of the document collection, servicers must retain detailed records of borrower solicitations or borrower-initiated inquiries regarding HAFA, the outcome of the evaluation for foreclosure alternatives under HAFA and specific justification with supporting details if foreclosure alternatives were denied. Records must also be retained to document the reasons for termination of the SSA or expiration of HAFA transactions without a completed short sale or acceptance of a DIL.

Signatures and Electronic Documents. All HAFA documentation must be signed by an authorized representative of the servicer and reflect the actual date of signature by the servicer's representative.

Unless a borrower or co-borrower is deceased or a borrower and a co-borrower are divorced, all parties who signed the original loan documents or their duly authorized representatives must execute the HAFA documents. If a borrower and a co-borrower are divorced and the property has been transferred to one spouse in the divorce decree, the spouse who no longer has an interest in the property is not required to execute the HAFA documents. Servicers may evaluate requests on a case-by-case basis when the borrower is unable to sign due to circumstances such as mental incapacity or military deployment.

Any party to a document utilized in HAFA may, subject to applicable law and any investor requirements or restrictions, prepare, sign and send the document through electronic means provided: (a) appropriate technology is used to store an authentic record of the executed document and the technology otherwise ensures the security, confidentiality and privacy of the transaction, (b) the document is enforceable under applicable law, (c) the servicer obtains the borrower's consent to use electronic means to enter into the document, (d) the servicer ensures that the borrower is able to retain a copy of the document and provides a copy to the borrower that the borrower may download, store and print, and (e) the borrower, at any time, may elect to enter into the document through paper means or to receive a paper copy of the document.

Reporting Requirements

As a condition to receiving the incentive payments offered through HAFA, servicers are required to provide periodic HAFA loan level data to Fannie Mae, in its capacity as program administrator. The data submitted must be accurate, complete, timely, and agree with the servicer's records. Data will be reported by a servicer at key milestones in the transaction:

HOW TO AVOID FLORIDA FORECLOSURE

· **Notification** – when the SSA or DIL Agreement is signed and executed, or updated following an extension of the marketing terms;

· **Short Sale/DIL Loan Set Up** – at the transfer of property ownership (closing of a short sale or acceptance of DIL); and/or

· **Termination** – when the SSA or DIL Agreement expires or when the SSA or DIL Agreement is terminated by the servicer.

Each milestone is a separate data transmission and must be reported no later than the fourth business day of the month following the event. The required data elements are attached to this Supplemental Directive as Exhibit D. In addition, HAFA reporting requirements will be posted on the servicer web portal at www.hmpadmin.com. Note also that the reporting information required under Schedule I and Schedule IV of Supplemental Directive 09-06 must be provided by the servicer for all HAFA transactions, including those that occur prior to April 5, 2010.

The HAFA reporting and payment processes are currently under development by Fannie Mae, in its capacity as program administrator. Subsequent guidance will be provided describing when the HAFA reporting and processes will be available. Servicers will not be required to report HAFA data until the reporting process is in place, but in this interim period servicers must collect and store information on all HAFA transactions so that the necessary data can be reported when the processes become available. In addition, HAFA incentives will not be paid until the payment process is available; borrowers, servicers and investors will be reimbursed for all incentives relating to HAFA transactions closed prior to the reporting and payment processes becoming available.

Credit Bureau Reporting. The servicer should continue to report a "full file" status to the major credit repositories for each loan under the HAFA program in accordance with the Fair Credit Reporting Act and the Consumer Data Industry Association's ("CDIA's") Metro 2 Format credit bureau requirements. "Full file" reporting means that the servicer must describe the exact Rating code should be the code that properly identifies whether the account is current or past due within the activity period being reported – prior to completion of the HAFA transaction. Because CDIA's Metro 2 format does not provide an Account Status Code allowable value for a short sale, a short sale should identified with the reporting of Special Comment Code "AU". The information below is consistent with "CDIA Mortgage and Home Equity Reporting Guidelines in Response to Current Financial Conditions" (May 2009).

Reporting should be as follows:

Short Sales

·   Account Status Code = 13 (paid or closed/zero balance)

·   Payment Rating = 0, 1, 2, 3, 4, 5, or 6

- Special Comment Code = AU (account paid in full for less than the full balance)
- Current Balance = $0
- Amount Past Due = $0
- Date Closed = MMDDYYYY
- Date of Last Payment = MMDDYYYY

Deed-in-Lieu

- Account Status Code = 89 (deed-in-lieu of foreclosure on a defaulted loan)
- Payment Rating = 0, 1, 2, 3, 4, 5, or 6
- Current Balance = $0
- Amount Past Due = $0
- Date Closed = MMDDYYYY
- Date of Last Payment = MMDDYYYY

Compliance

Servicers must comply with the HAFA short sale and DIL requirements specified in this Supplemental Directive and any subsequent policy guidance. Servicers must have adequate staffing and resources for responding to borrower requests for participation, for receiving and processing HAFA documents in accordance with program guidelines and for ensuring that inquiries and complaints about HAFA receive fair consideration, along with timely and appropriate response and resolution.

Treasury has selected Freddie Mac to serve as its compliance agent for HAFA. In its role as compliance agent, Freddie Mac will utilize Freddie Mac employees and contractors to conduct independent compliance assessments. The scope of the assessments will include, among other things, an evaluation of documented evidence to confirm adherence (e.g., accuracy and timeliness) to HAFA requirements with respect to the following:

·   Assessment of the process for evaluating and approving borrowers for a HAFA short sale or DIL.

Adherence to the standard policies and guidelines for completing HAFA short sales and DIL and consistent application of same.

·   Determining fair market value, recommended list price, approved sale proceeds and approved minimum net proceeds, as applicable.

·   Guidelines for allowable payoffs to junior lien holders.

·   Use of standard documents and document retention.

·   Completion of borrower, servicer and investor incentive payments.

The review will also confirm the existence and evaluate the effectiveness of the servicer's quality assurance program; such evaluation will include, without limitation, the timing and size of the sample selection, the scope of the quality assurance reviews, and the reporting and remediation process.

HOW TO AVOID FLORIDA FORECLOSURE

There will be two types of compliance assessments: on-site and remote. Both on-site and remote reviews will include the following activities (among others): notification, scheduling, selfassessments, documentation submission, interviews, file reviews, and reporting.

For on-site reviews, Freddie Mac will strive to provide the servicer with (i) a 30-day advance notification of a pending review and (ii) subsequent confirmation of the dates of the review; however, Freddie Mac reserves the right to arrive at the servicer's site unannounced. Freddie Mac will request the servicer to make available documentation, including, without limitation, policies and procedures, management reports, loan files and a risk control self assessment ready for review. Moreover, Freddie Mac may request additional loan files during the review.

Interviews will usually be conducted in-person. During the review window, Freddie Mac will review loan files and other requested documentation to evaluate compliance with HAFA terms. Upon the completion of the review, Freddie Mac will conduct an exit interview with the servicer to discuss preliminary assessment results.

For remote reviews, Freddie Mac will request the servicer to send documentation, including, without limitation, policies and procedures, management reports, loan files and a risk control self assessment within 30 calendar days of the request. In addition, time will be scheduled for phone interviews, including a results summary call after the compliance review is completed to discuss preliminary results.

The targeted time frame for publishing the servicer assessment report is 30 calendar days after the completion of the review. Treasury will receive a copy of the report five business days prior to the release of the report to the servicer. There will be an issue/resolution appeal process for servicer assessments. Servicers will be able to submit concerns or disputes to an independent quality assurance team within Freddie Mac.

A draft rating and implication methodology for the compliance assessments will be published in a subsequent Supplemental Directive and servicer feedback will be solicited prior to the finalization of the methodology.

HOW TO AVOID FLORIDA FORECLOSURE

HOW TO AVOID FLORIDA FORECLOSURE

HOW TO AVOID FLORIDA FORECLOSURE

About the Author

Mark Galbraith is currently a licensed Realtor® and a licensed Mortgage Broker.

Upon leaving Northwestern University, Mark immediately became a Loan Officer for a Chicago based bank. Mark specialized in commercial loans and SBA loans assisting individuals who had a business dream. He obtained his real estate license due to persuasion from his father who did commercial real estate for 43 years and his mother who did residential real estate for 22 years. During the housing market bust he has turned his attention to those homeowners who have become disillusioned with their "American Dream".

To contact Mark by e-mail: markgalbraith@gmail.com

By Phone: (813) 333-1092

HOW TO AVOID FLORIDA FORECLOSURE

www.ingramcontent.com/pod-product-compliance
Lightning Source LLC
Chambersburg PA
CBHW072132280526
45788CB00002B/604